THINGS TH FLOAT

Devised and written by
Robin Wright

Designed and illustrated by
Teresa Foster

Edited by Tony Potter

Contents

About This Book	2
About Things That Float	3
Making Things That Float	4
Things You Need	5
Dolphins	6
Summer Swimmers	8
Corkodile	10
Windsurfer	12
Paddle Boat	14
Octopus	16
Frogman	18
Peller Boat	20
Submarine	22
Patterns	24

About This Book

Dolphins *

This book shows you how to make lots of things that float. There are boats and a submarine, an octopus and even some leaping dolphins!

The pictures on this page show you all the things you can make.

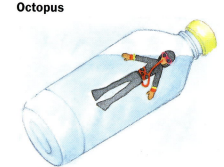
Octopus *

Summer Swimmers

Everything is made from ordinary things that you might find around the house, like corks and pieces of packaging. There are lists of things you need on every page.

Frogman

Corkodile

There are simple step-by-step instructions and patterns at the back of the book, to make it easy to draw and cut out any difficult shapes.

You might need help from a grown-up for things marked with a star like this: *

Peller Boat

Windsurfer

Paddle Boat

Submarine

About Things That Float

◄ Things which are lighter than water, such as wood or cork, will float. Boats or fishing floats are often made of these materials.

Something which is heavier than water, such as metal or Plasticine, will sink. ►

◄ Air can make things float which are heavier than water. If air is trapped inside a heavy container, it will help it to float. Air helps to make things buoyant – which means able to float.

The more air there is inside an object, the more buoyant it will be. ►

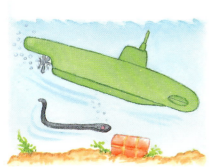

◄ Submarines sink because the air is pumped out of their tanks and replaced with water. To make them float their tanks have to be filled with air.

Boats made of material heavier than water – such as steel – are made to float because of their shape. ►

Making Things That Float

There are patterns to trace or photocopy at the back of this book.

Put things on a wooden board to cut them with a craft knife. Don't cut directly on to the table.

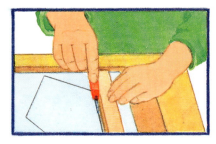

Be very careful when cutting with a craft knife. Use an old wooden ruler to cut against.

Always ask a grown-up to help you cut anything you find difficult.

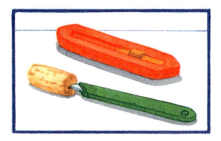

Push the craft knife blade into a cork when you finish. The blade on some knives goes back into the handle.

Try to be neat and tidy. Clear up the tools and materials when you have finished working.

Make sure you wash your brushes out and replace lids on pots when you have finished.

Make sure that the glue and paints are dry before you try out the things you have made.

Check with a grown-up before filling a bath or basin with water to test that things float properly.

Things You Need

You should be able to buy some or all of these things from a craft or model shop if you do not have them at home.

- craft knife
- pencil
- ruler
- scissors

This page show you all the tools and materials you need to make everything in this book.

Some things are more difficult to make than others, so it is a good idea to ask a grown up for help if you get stuck.

- waterproof glue
- waterproof paints
- polystyrene tiles
- plastic cartons
- plastic sheets or tissue
- elastic strips (from a model shop)
- rubber bands
- wool
- cotton reels
- glass beads
- wooden beads
- used matchsticks
- Plasticine
- cotton
- ping-pong balls
- corks
- wire
- a cardboard tube from a roll of kitchen paper or foil
- waterproof sticky tape
- balloon
- an empty washing-up liquid bottle
- drinking straws
- thin plastic tube (from a model shop)
- an empty 1-2 litre clear plastic bottle
- a plastic propeller (from a model shop)
- a plastic pen top

Dolphins

Leaping, floating, altogether,
Dolphins swim in any weather.
Kind and clever, gentle too,
They'll very soon make friends with you.

What you need

- a polystyrene tile
- paper
- a pencil
- scissors
- a craft knife
- waterproof glue
- 6 glass beads
- waterproof paint
- a ping-pong ball
- Plasticine

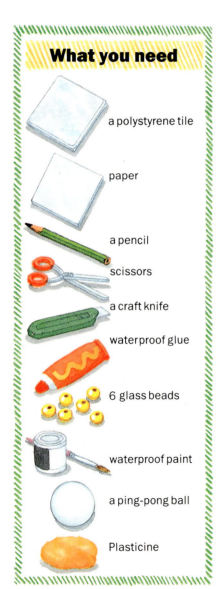

1 Trace the shapes of the dolphins on to a piece of paper. Cut them out with a pair of scissors.

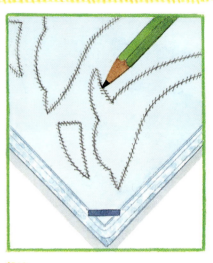

2 Using the cut-out shapes draw the outlines of the bodies, fins and tails on to a polystyrene tile.

3 Very carefully, cut out the shapes of the bodies, fins and tails from polystyrene with a craft knife.

4 Glue the fins and tails to the bodies. Glue on glass beads for eyes. Paint the Dolphins with waterproof paint.

The patterns for the Dolphins are on page 24

5 Glue the Dolphins together. You can arrange them in any way you like.

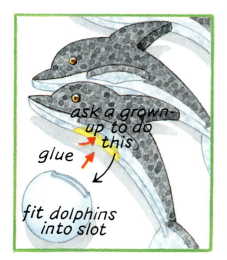

6 Ask a grown-up to cut a slot in a ping-pong ball. Glue the lowest dolphin into the slot.

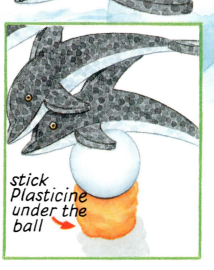

7 Stick a lump of Plasticine on the ping-pong ball so that the Dolphins float upright.

How they float

The air in the ping-pong ball makes it float. The Plasticine is heavier than water and tries to sink. This makes the ball float so that the dolphins stay upright. You may have to experiment until you get the balance just right.

Summer Swimmers

1 Paint various skin colours and faces on the corks. It's a good idea to give them different expressions.

What you need

- corks
- wool
- Plasticine
- used matchsticks
- an empty clear plastic bottle
- waterproof sticky tape
- waterproof paints
- waterproof glue
- a plastic carton
- drinking straws

2 Cut some short lengths of wool and unravel them to make the hair. Glue it to the corks. Paint on costumes.

The patterns for the Swimmers' hands, feet and masks are on page 25.

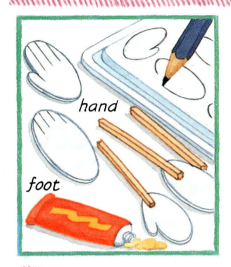

3 Trace the shapes of the hands and feet on to plastic or card and glue them on to matchsticks.

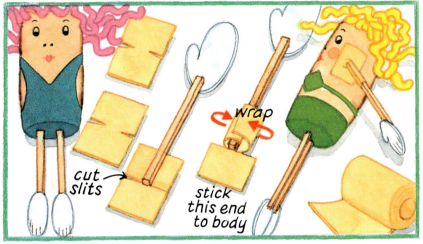

4 Cut small squares of sticky tape and make small slits in them. Wrap one end round the matchstick arms. Stick the arms to the bodies with the other end of the tape. Make holes in the corks and glue in the legs.

5 You can make masks from pieces of clear plastic. Cut and glue drinking straws to make snorkels.

6 To make the swimmers float properly, stick small lumps of Plasticine on the sides or ends of the corks.

Why they swim

Cork is lighter than water, so it floats. The Plasticine weight makes one side or end of the cork heavier than the other. The heaviest part of the corks will sink below the surface of the water, making them swim or stand upright.

Corkodile

1 Place four corks in a line. Join them together by gluing a piece of string to them.

What you need

- corks
- string
- scissors
- waterproof glue
- plastic carton
- waterproof paint
- Plasticine
- glass beads

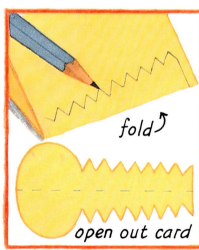

2 Fold a piece of thin card and trace on the head and jaw shapes. Cut them out and unfold the paper.

The patterns for the Corkodile are on page 25

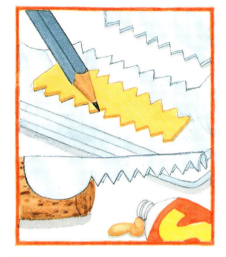
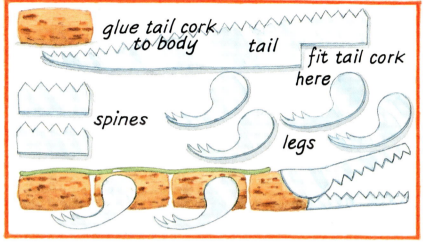

3 Draw round the shapes on a piece of plastic carton. Cut them out and glue them to one end of the body.

4 Draw the leg, tail and spine shapes on to a piece of thin card. Trace them on to some plastic carton and then cut them out. Glue the legs to the two middle corks as shown in the picture above.

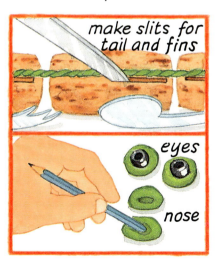

Why it works

The Corkodile's body is lighter than water, so it floats. The small pieces of Plasticine inside each of the feet make the heaviest part of the Corkodile stay under the surface of the water. If you push him over, he'll roll back again!

5 Make slits in the corks and glue in the spines and tail. Use glass beads for eyes and Plasticine for a nose.

6 Stick on the eyes with Plasticine, then paint the Corkodile. Put a piece of Plasticine on each foot.

Windsurfer

What you need

- a polystyrene tile
- a craft knife
- a piece of card
- scissors
- waterproof glue
- waterproof paints
- a thin plastic bag
- 2 drinking straws
- cotton or thread
- a small piece of plastic from a food carton.

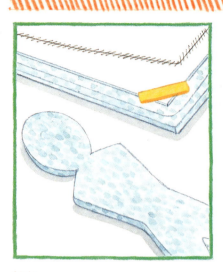

1 Trace the body and board shapes on to paper. Tape them to a polystyrene tile and cut them out.

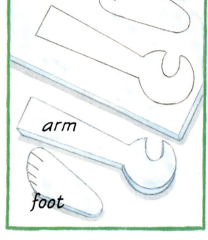

2 Trace the surfer's arms and feet on to a piece of card and cut them out. Mark in the toes.

3 Glue the arms to the body and the feet to the legs. Paint on the surfer's face and also the wet suit.

4 Cut the shape of the sail from a piece of thin plastic bag. Bend a drinking straw and glue the sail to it.

The patterns for the Windsurfer are on pages 26 and 27

tie ends

5 Bend a straw round the mast to make the boom and tie the ends together. Hook the surfer's hands on the boom.

hook arms on to boom

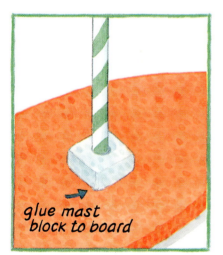
glue mast block to board

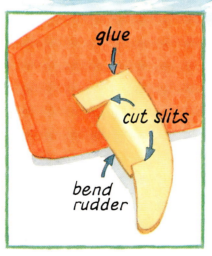
glue
cut slits
bend rudder

How it works

Twist the mast and bend the rudder so that they are on the same side of the board. Wind in the sail pushes the board one way, while water on the rudder turns it the other. When they are balanced the board will sail in a straight line.

6 Cut the mast block from polystyrene. Glue it to the board. Make a hole and push in the mast. Do not glue it.

7 Trace the keel and rudder shape on to a piece of plastic and cut it out. Glue it to the underneath of the board.

Paddle Boat

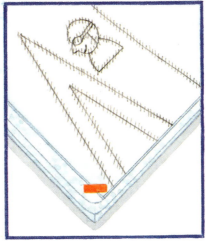

1 Trace the shapes of the driver, cockpit and hull and cut them out of polystyrene.

2 Glue the cockpit and driver to the hull using waterproof glue.

What you need

- polystyrene tile
- craft knife
- waterproof glue
- clear plastic
- waterproof paint
- a rubber band
- plastic card
- cotton
- waterproof tape

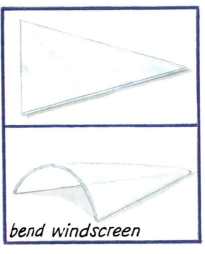

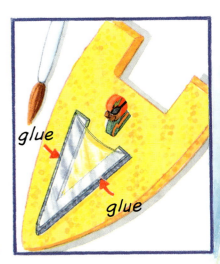

3 Cut the windscreen out of a piece of clear plastic, and bend it to fit the cockpit.

4 Glue the windscreen to the cockpit. Then paint the driver and the boat.

The patterns for the Paddle Boat are on pages 28 and 29

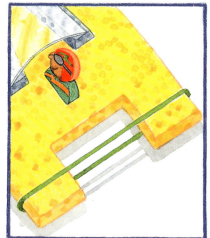

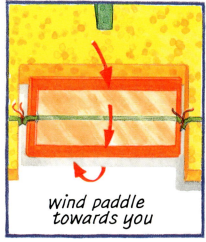

5 Put a rubber band round the ends of the boat. Cut the paddle from a piece of stiff plastic.

6 Tape the paddle between the rubber band. Tie cotton round each side of the rubber band.

7 Turn the paddle towards you about a dozen times to twist the rubber band. Hold it until the boat goes in the water.

How it works

Put the Paddle Boat into the water, then let the paddle go. As the rubber band unwinds the paddle blades turn and push against the water so that the boat moves forward.

Octopus

What you need

- a ping-pong ball
- pencil
- craft knife
- 2 wooden beads
- waterproof paint
- glue
- 1 × 88cm length of elastic
- 1 × 1m length of thin plastic tube (from a model shop)
- Plasticine

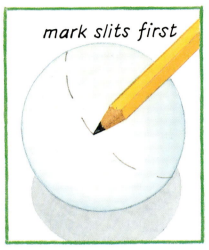

1 Make eight marks with a pencil round the middle of the ping-pong ball.

2 Ask an adult to make small slits at each mark using a craft knife.

3 Paint the ball with waterproof paint and glue on two wooden beads for eyes.

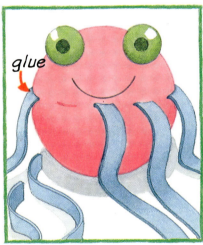

4 Cut eight 11cm lengths of elastic and glue them into the slots in the body.

The pattern for the Octopus is on page 29

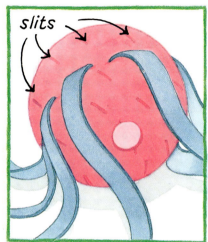

5 Ask an adult to make small slits all over the ball, and one hole underneath big enough to take the tube.

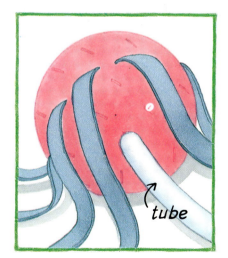

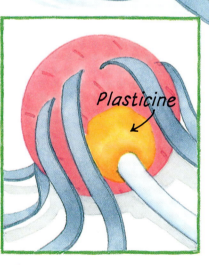

6 Push the tube into the hole underneath the ball and glue it into place.

7 Wrap a piece of Plasticine round the tube next to the ball.

How it works

Put the Octopus into a basin full of water and it will sink as the water fills the body. Blow into the tube, and the octopus will swim up to the surface. This is because by blowing you fill the ball with air. This makes it buoyant so that it floats.

Frogman

What you need

- plastic from a food carton.
- scissors
- waterproof paints
- Plasticine
- a pen top
- 2 rubber bands
- an empty 1-2 litre plastic bottle

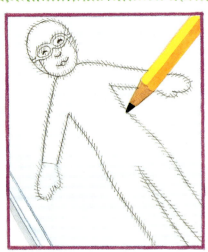

1 Trace the shape of the frogman onto a piece of plastic from a food carton.

2 Cut it out and paint the face and body with waterproof paint.

make sure the opening is clear

3 Wrap a lump of Plasticine round the pen top. Don't block up the open end.

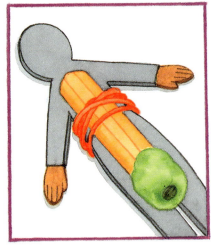

4 Attach the pen top to the frogman's back with an elastic band.

The pattern for the Frogman is on page 31

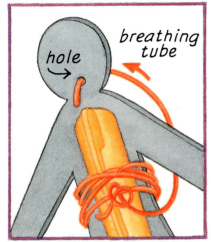

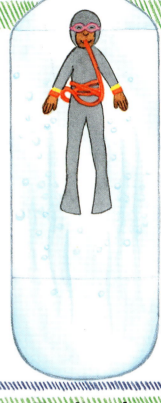

5 Make a hole in the frogman's mouth and push in a cut rubber band for a breathing tube. Glue it into place.

6 Fill the bottle with water, leaving a small space. Push the frogman into the bottle and screw on the cap.

7 The diver floats because a small air space is trapped inside the pen top.

8 Now squeeze the bottle and the diver will sink to the bottom.

How it works

When you squeeze the bottle it makes more water fill the pen top. As the air space is smaller, it cannot support the Frogman and he sinks. Release the bottle and the Frogman will rise to the surface as the pen top fills with air again.

Peller Boat

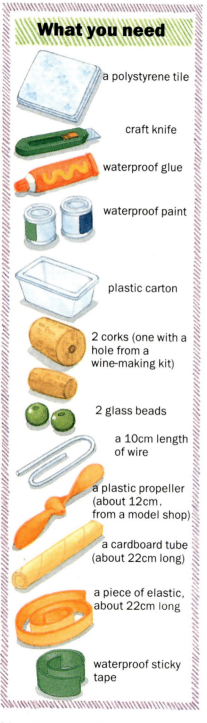

What you need

- a polystyrene tile
- craft knife
- waterproof glue
- waterproof paint
- plastic carton
- 2 corks (one with a hole from a wine-making kit)
- 2 glass beads
- a 10cm length of wire
- a plastic propeller (about 12cm, from a model shop)
- a cardboard tube (about 22cm long)
- a piece of elastic, about 22cm long
- waterproof sticky tape

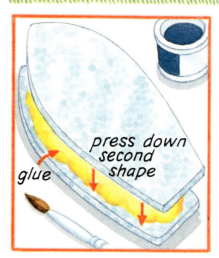

1 Trace two hull shapes on to polystyrene. Cut them out and glue them together.

2 Make the cabin from a carton. Glue it to the hull. Paint the boat, with windows on the cabin.

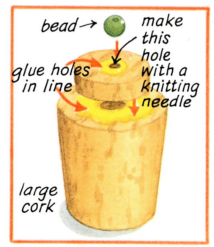

3 Cut a 1cm piece of cork and glue it to the big cork. Make a hole through both and glue on a glass bead.

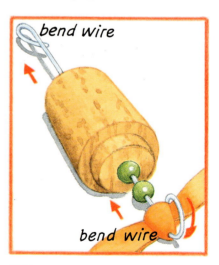

4 Push the wire through the bead and corks. Slide on the other bead and propeller. Bend the ends of the wire as shown.

The pattern for the Peller Boat is on page 30

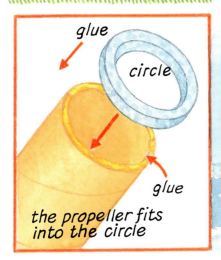

5 Glue a polystyrene circle to the cardboard tube so that it fits the cork holding the propeller.

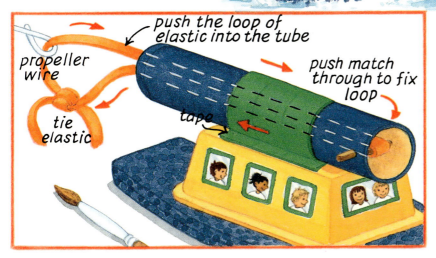

How it works

Wind the propeller anti-clockwise. Place the boat in water and let the propeller go. As the propeller turns, its blades cut through the air and push the boat forward.

6 Push the elastic through the wire and tie the ends. Push the loop through the tube and fix it with a match. Fix the propeller tube to the cabin top with sticky tape and glue. Make sure the propeller clears the hull. Then paint the tube.

Submarine

What you need

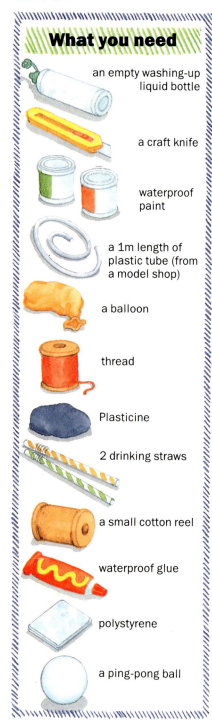

- an empty washing-up liquid bottle
- a craft knife
- waterproof paint
- a 1m length of plastic tube (from a model shop)
- a balloon
- thread
- Plasticine
- 2 drinking straws
- a small cotton reel
- waterproof glue
- polystyrene
- a ping-pong ball

remove cap — ask a grown-up to do this

1 Very carefully using a craft knife, cut slits into the side of the plastic bottle, to make the hull of the submarine.

bend out long flaps

2 Open the slits out, and bend back the two longest flaps. Paint the bottle with waterproof paint.

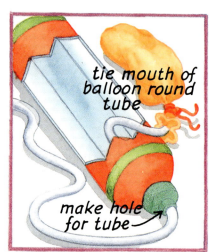

tie mouth of balloon round tube

make hole for tube

3 Push the tube through the spout of the bottle. Tie a balloon round the other end of the tube.

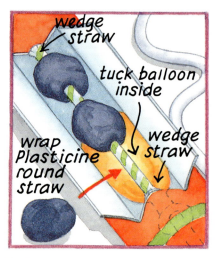

wedge straw

tuck balloon inside

wrap Plasticine round straw

wedge straw

4 Tuck the balloon into the bottle. Wrap Plasticine round a straw and wedge it between the points in the slot.

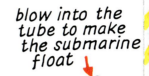

5 Cut a hole in the hull. Glue in the conning tower, made from a cotton reel with a straw for the periscope.

blow into the tube to make the submarine float

6 Half a ping-pong ball glued to a circle of polystyrene will make the nose. Glue the nose to the hull.

7 Make small slits in the ping-pong ball; also round the ends of the bottle. Use a craft knife or scissors.

How it works

Put the submarine into a bath of water. It will sink as it fills with water. Blow into the tube and the submarine will surface. The amount of air in the balloon buoyancy tank controls the depth at which the submarine floats in the water. This is how a real submarine works.

Patterns

Dolphins

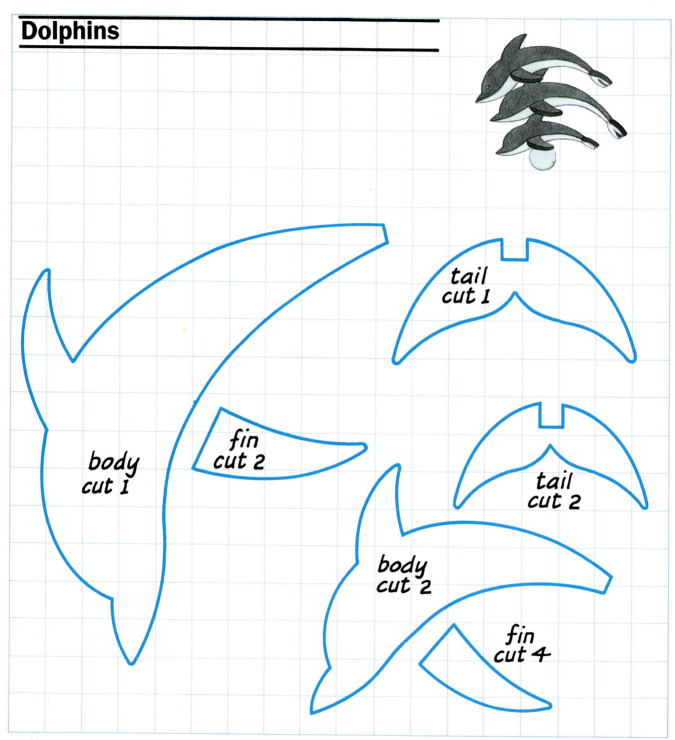

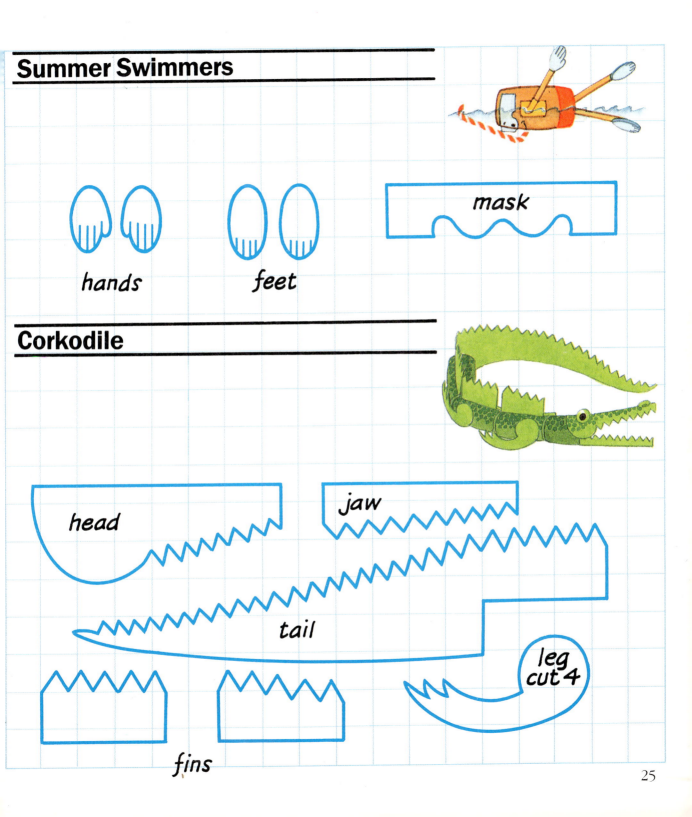

Windsurfer

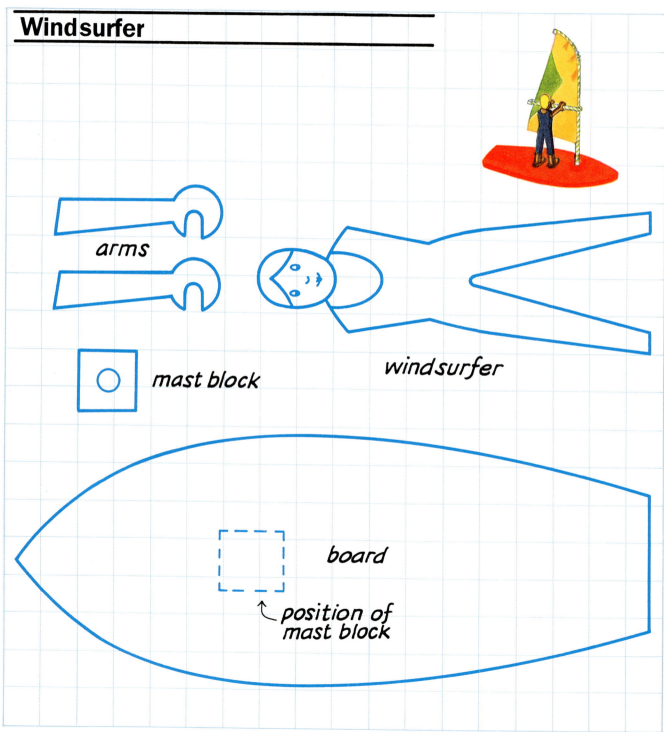

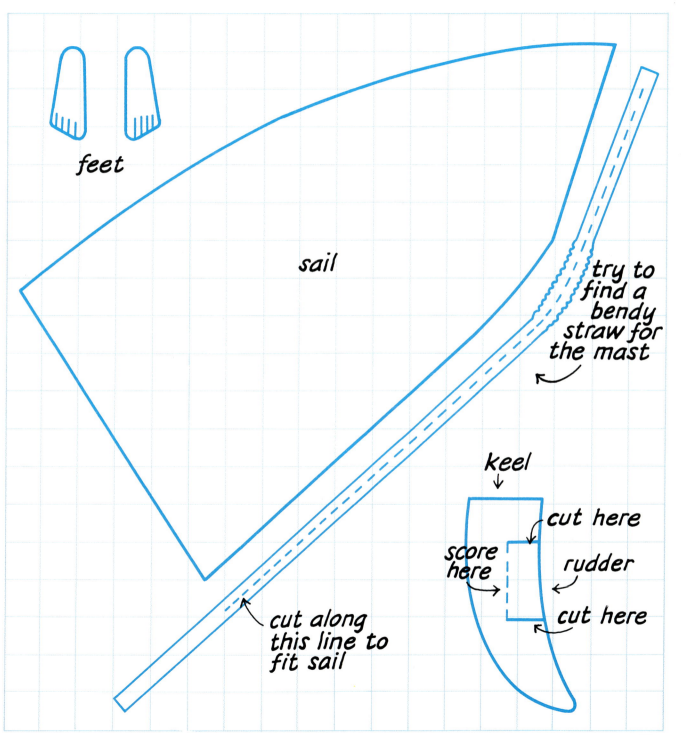

Paddle Boat

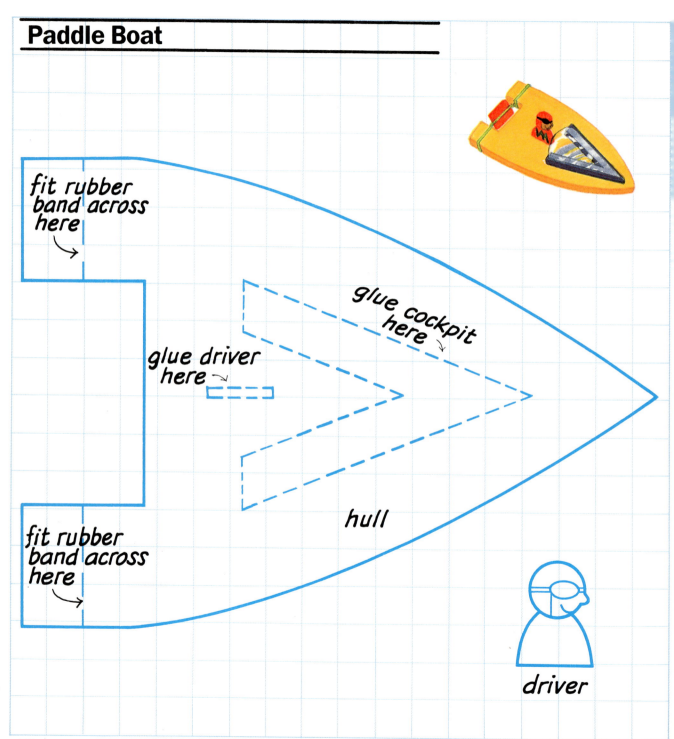

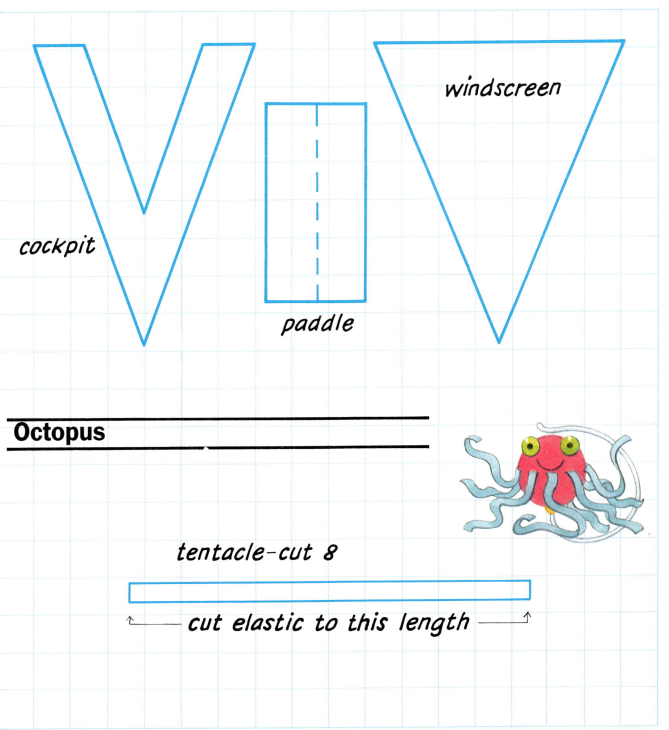

Peller Boat

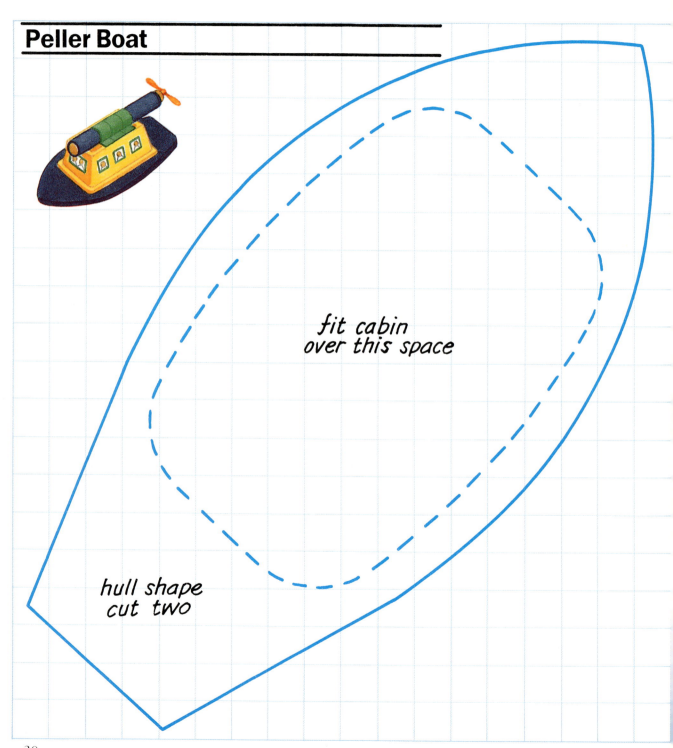

fit cabin over this space

hull shape cut two

Frogman

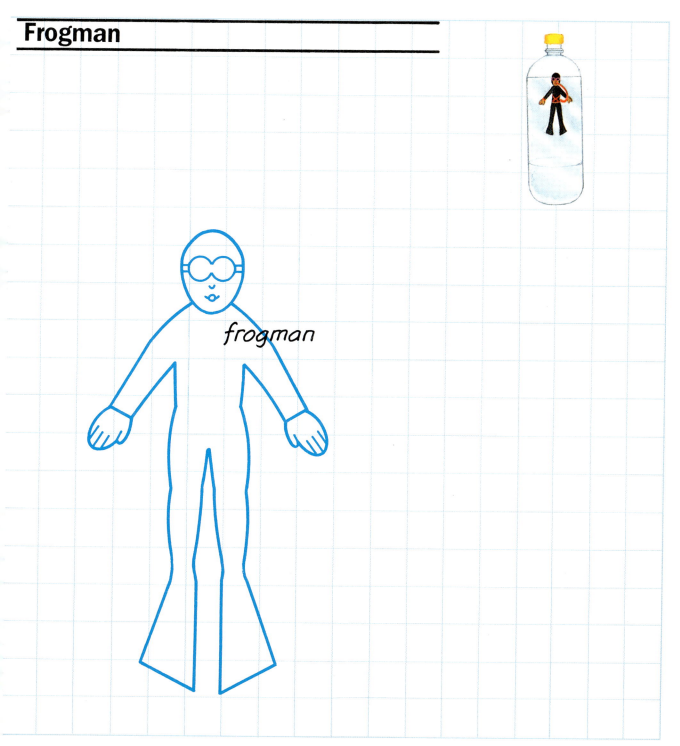

William Collins Sons & Co Ltd
London • Glasgow • Sydney • Auckland
Toronto • Johannesburg

First published 1990
©William Collins Sons & Co Ltd 1990

A CIP catalogue record for this book is available from the
British Library

ISBN 0 00 190029 3 (Hardback)
ISBN 0 00 190061 7 (Paperback)

All rights reserved. No part of this publication may be reproduced, stored in a retrieval system, or transmitted, in any form or by any means, electronic, mechanical, photocopying, recording or otherwise, without the prior permission of William Collins Sons & Co Ltd, 8 Grafton Street, London W1X 3LA.

Printed in Portugal by Resopal